To: From:

On the occasion of:

I Am of Ireland

A photographic celebration by Cyril A. Reilly and Renée Travis Reilly

Winston Press

Copyright © 1981 by Cyril A. Reilly and Renée Travis Reilly
All rights reserved. No part of this book may be reproduced or
used in any form without written permission from Winston Press, Inc.

Library of Congress Catalog Card Number: 80-53559
ISBN: 0-03-059058-2

Art Direction and Photo Editing: Keith McCormick and Miriam Frost

Printed in the United States of America.

5   4   3   2

Winston Press, Inc.
430 Oak Grove
Minneapolis, Minnesota 55403

BEV

Acknowledgments

To the best of our knowledge all poems quoted, except those listed below, are in the public domain. We apologize for errors or unintentional omissions of acknowledgments due; they will be corrected in future printings. We are grateful for permission to reprint these copyrighted materials:

"Bring Home the Poet," "A Soft Day," "The Viking Terror," "Columcille's Greeting to Ireland," "The Heavenly Pilot," "The Old Woman," "I See His Blood upon the Rose," "The Love-Talker": Reprinted with permission of the Devin-Adair Company, Old Greenwich, Conn. 06870, from *1000 Years of Irish Poetry*, edited by Kathleen Hoagland. Copyright 1947 by the Devin-Adair Company; renewed 1975. Our special thanks to Devin A. Garrity, president of Devin-Adair, for his generous help.

"A Faery Song": Reprinted with permission of Macmillan Publishing Co., Inc., from *Collected Poems* by William Butler Yeats. Copyright 1906 by Macmillan Publishing Co., Inc.; renewed 1934 by W.B. Yeats.

"The Wild Swans at Coole": Reprinted with permission of Macmillan Publishing Co., Inc., from *Collected Poems* by William Butler Yeats. Copyright 1919 by Macmillan Publishing Co., Inc.; renewed 1947 by Bertha Georgie Yeats.

"Tom the Lunatic": Reprinted with permission of Macmillan Publishing Co., Inc., from *Collected Poems* by William Butler Yeats. Copyright 1933 by Macmillan Publishing Co., Inc.; renewed 1961 by Bertha Georgie Yeats.

"Valediction": Reprinted with permission of Faber and Faber, Ltd., from *The Collected Poems of Louis MacNeice.* Copyright 1949, 1966.

"The Twilight of Earth": Reprinted with permission of Russell & Volkening, Inc., from *Collected Poems* by AE (George Russell). Copyright 1913 by Macmillan & Co., Ltd.; second edition 1926.

"Father Matt": Reprinted with permission of St. Martin's Press, Inc., from *A Soul for Sale,* by Patrick Kavanagh. Copyright 1947 by Macmillan Publishing Co., Ltd.

"The Abdication of Fergus MacRoy": Reprinted in *An Anthology of Irish Literature,* edited by David H. Greene. Random House, Inc. Copyright 1954.

I Am of Ireland

Freely and slowly the first time.
Repeat as desired, increasing the tempo.

Words adapted
Music by Cyril A. Reilly

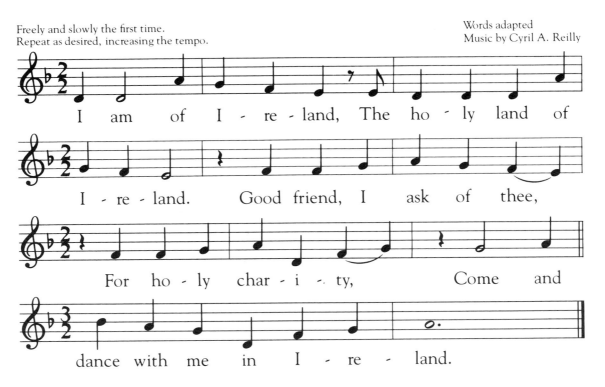

I am of I - re - land, The ho - ly land of

I - re - land. Good friend, I ask of thee,

For ho - ly char - i - ty, Come and

dance with me in I - re - land.

—"I Am of Ireland," anon. (c. 1300-1350); adapted

Come and dance with me in Ireland...

Sheila Berney, Dublin

I will make my journey,
if life and health but stand,
Unto that pleasant country,
that fresh and fragrant strand,
. . . the fair hills of holy Ireland.

—"The Fair Hills of Ireland," anon. (18th c.); transl. Samuel Ferguson

There lies that fairy-land of mine . . .

—"Dreams," Cecil Francis Alexander

Teelin Bay

A nation free and grand...

—"God Save Ireland," Timothy Daniel O'Sullivan

Left: Harry (The Boat) McIlhaney, Downings
Right: South of Gortahork

We're children of a fighting race,
That never yet has known disgrace.

—"The Soldier's Song," Peadar Kearney

Left: Teenagers at Charleville,
County Cork
Right: Patrick Wilson, Charleville,
County Cork

Yeats's grave,
Drumcliffe

Bring home the poet, laurel-crowned,
Lay him to rest in Irish ground;
Make him a grave near Sligo Bay,
At fair Drumcliffe or Knocknarea,
For near his mother's kindred dwelt,
And at Drumcliffe his fathers knelt,
And all about in beauty's haze,
The print of proud, heroic days,
With wind and wave in druid hymn
To chant for aye his requiem.
And he'll have mourners at his bier,
The fairy hosts who hold him dear,
And Father Gilligan, he'll be there,
The martial Maeve and Deirdre fair,
And lads he knew in town and glen,
The fisher folk and sailor men;
The Dooney fiddler and the throng
He made immortal with his song;
And proud in grief his rightful queen,
Ni Houlihan, the brave Kathleen.
Bring home the poet, let him rest
In the old land he loved the best.

—"Bring Home the Poet," Patrick MacDonough

In Dublin's fair city...

—"Molly Malone" (folk song)

Left: St. Stephen's Green, Dublin
Above: Patricia Coffey and child, Dublin
Right: Georgian homes, Dublin

Abbey River, Limerick
Far right: Angler's festival,
Downings

I long for the dear old river,
Where I dreamed my youth away;
For a dreamer lives forever,
And a toiler dies in a day.

—"The Cry of the Dreamer," John Boyle O'Reilly

Tis the bells of Shandon
  That sound so grand on
The pleasant waters
  Of the river Lee.

—"The Shandon Bells," Francis S. Mahony (Father Prout)

The great waves of the Atlantic sweep storming on the way,
Shining green and silver with the hidden herring shoal,
But the Little Waves of Breffny have drenched my heart in spray,
And the Little Waves of Breffny go stumbling through my soul.

—"The Little Waves of Breffny," Eva Gore-Booth

North of Ballyconnell,
County Cavan

The fair fields
our children's feet
shall tread...

—"The Memory of the Dead (1798)," John Kells Ingram

Michael and Mary Theresa
Cannon, Glengesh
Right: Dingle Peninsula,
County Kerry

So simple is the earth we tread,
   So quick with love and life her frame,
Ten thousand years have dawned and fled,
   And still her magic is the same.

—"The Earth and Man," Stopford A. Brooke

Mary A. Gillespie,
Sheegus, Ballyshannon,
Far right: Charlie Browne,
Olde Glen Tavern

A land where even the old are fair,
And even the wise are merry of tongue...

—"A Faery Song" (from *The Land of Heart's Desire*), William Butler Yeats

. . . the green gush of Irish spring

—"Valediction," Louis MacNeice

County Westmeath

A soft day, thank God!
The hills wear a shroud
Of silver cloud;
The web the spider weaves
Is a glittering net;

The woodland path is wet,
And the soaking earth smells sweet,
Under my two bare feet,
And the rain drips,
Drips, drips, drips from the leaves.

—"A Soft Day," Winifred M. Letts

Now they drift on the still water
     Mysterious, beautiful;
Among what rushes will they build,
By what lake's edge or pool
Delight men's eyes when I awake some day
To find they have flown away?

—"The Wild Swans at Coole," William Butler Yeats

Left: County Sligo
Above: Near Dunfanaghy

He was a part of the place,
Natural as a round stone in a grass field...

—"Father Matt," Patrick Kavanagh

William Fox
digging turf near
Bray, County Wicklow

Green, in the wizard arms
of the foam-bearded Atlantic...

—"The Banshee," John Todhunter

Achill Island,
County Mayo

Fierce is the wind tonight,
  It ploughs up the white hair of the sea.
I have no fear that the Viking hosts
Will come over the water to me.

—"The Viking Terror," anon. (8th or 9th c.); transl. F. N. Robinson

Falcarragh Strand

The salt main where the sea-gulls cry...

—"Columcille's Greeting to Ireland," attributed to St. Columcille
(12th c.); transl. William Reeves and Kuno Meyer

Wilt Thou steer my frail black bark
O'er the dark ocean's foam?
Wilt Thou come, Lord, to my boat,
Where afloat, my will would roam?

—"The Heavenly Pilot," Cormac (9th-10th c.); transl. George Sigerson

Above and at right:
Killybegs Harbor

The sea is full, delightful is the home of ships...

—"Song of the Sea," attributed to Rumann MacColmain (11th c.);
transl. Kuno Meyer

The hidden light
the spirit owns...

—"The Twilight of Earth," AE (George Russell)

The Celtic Cross that marks our fatherland...
Druids and Danes and Saxons vainly rage
Around its base;
It standeth shock on shock, and age on age,
Star of our scattered race.

—"The Celtic Cross," Thomas D'Arcy McGee

We invoke holy Patrick, Ireland's chief apostle.
Glorious is his wondrous name, a flame that baptized heathen;
He warred against hard-hearted wizards.
He thrust down the mighty with the help of our Lord of fair heaven.
He purified Ireland's meadow-lands, a mighty birth.

—"Prayer of St. Patrick," Ninine (8th c.); transl.
Whitley Stokes and John Strachan

I wish, O Son of the living God,
O ancient, eternal King,
For a hidden little hut in the wilderness
That it may be my dwelling.

— "The Hermit's Song," anon. (9th c.); transl. Kuno Meyer

Beehive hut,
Dingle Peninsula,
County Kerry

Oh King of stars!
  Whether my house be dark or bright,
Never shall it be closed against any one,
Lest Christ close His house against me.

—"Hospitality in Ancient Ireland," anon. (13th c.)

Left: Near Bloody Foreland
Above: John Logue, Downings

As a white candle
In a holy place,
So is the beauty
Of an aged face.

As the spent radiance
Of the winter sun,
So is a woman
With her travail done.   —"The Old Woman," Joseph Campbell

All pathways by his feet are worn,
His strong heart stirs the ever-beating sea,
His crown of thorns is twined with every thorn,
His cross is every tree.

—"I See His Blood upon the Rose," Joseph Mary Plunkett

Left: Mrs. McClafferty, Balure
Right: South of Gweedore

Far left: Near Dunfanaghy
Below: Edward Coyle,
Downings

Whatever stands in field or flood,
    Bird, beast, fish or man,
Mare or stallion, cock or hen,
Stands in God's unchanging eye
In all the vigour of its blood;
In that faith I live or die.

—"Tom the Lunatic,"
William Butler Yeats

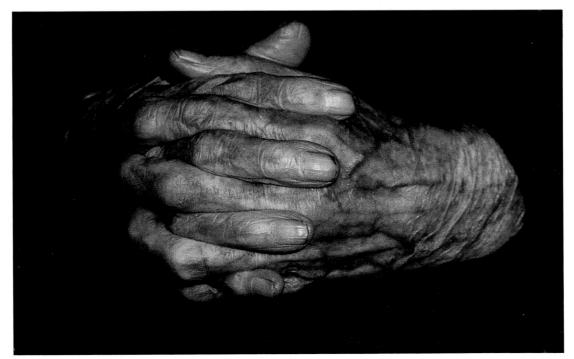

I rest with Thee, O Jesus,
And do Thou rest with me.
The oil of Christ on my poor soul,
The creed of the Twelve to make me whole,
Above my head I see.
O Father, who created me,
O Son, who purchased me,
O Spirit blest, who blessest me,
Rest ye with me.

—"Prayer," anon. (traditional)

A plenteous place
is Ireland
for hospitable cheer...

—"The Fair Hills of Ireland," anon. (18th c.)

Left: John Boyle,
Ballykilduff, Clooney
Above: Owen Gallagher,
Meenmore, Dungloe
Right: McClafferty brothers,
Balure
Below: Christina Cannon,
Ballyness

I'll never forget him—
    himself and his brogue,
And the comical gleam in his eye,
    the old rogue!
For 'twas he that could talk,
    in those days, with the best;
And you'd laugh at his jokes
    till you'd fear for your vest.
And you'd never grow tired
    of the wonderful flow
Of the language that came
    from the man from Mayo.

The story of Ireland—
    he knew it by heart,
And 'tis often he'd speak
    about Cormac MacArt,
Or of Brian Boru
    and his battles of old,
Or of Malachi
    wearing his collar of gold,
And of Daniel O'Connell—
    I almost would split
At the samples he gave
    of the Counsellor's wit.

But 'twas Emmet he loved
    and how grave he would grow
When that martyr was mentioned—
    the man from Mayo.

—"The Tailor That Came from Mayo," Denis A. McCarthy

Far left: Bernard Drummond,
Ballyshannon
Left: Dublin group
Below: Michael McBride,
Olde Glen Tavern

Here's brandy! Come, fill up your tumbler;
Or ale, if your liking be humbler;
    And while you've a shilling,
    Keep filling and swilling—
A fig for the growls of the grumbler!

—"O'Tuomy's Drinking Song," John O'Tuomy

The thoughts that we thought when young...

—"Early Thoughts," William Edward Hartpole Lecky

The memory of the brightest joys
In childhood's happy morn...

—"Know Ye Not That Lovely River," Gerald Griffin

Far left: Crossmalina, County Mayo
Left: Darron McCrory, Strabane,
County Tyrone
Right: Gerald McGloyn, Sheegus,
Ballyshannon
Below: McFadden children, Brinlack
Lower right: Geraldine Caldwell,
Donegal Town

*Y*ou are full of unshaped dreams...
You are laden with beginnings...

—"Wind in the Alleys," Lola Ridge

Left: Children at wedding,
Ardara
Above: Matthew Donovan,
Sandy Cove, County Dublin

Left: Deirdre Giblin,
Dalkey, County Dublin
Right: Deirdre Giblin
with Diarmuid MacGiolla Ruaidh,
Ballymun, Dublin

Girl of the red mouth,
Love me! Love me!
Girl of the red mouth,
Love me!

—"Girl of the Red Mouth," Martin MacDermott

If thou hadst known but half
Of the joyance of her laugh,
Of the measures of her walk,
Or the music of her talk,

Of the witch'ry of her wit,
Even when smarting under it, —
Half the sense, the charm, the grace,
Thou hadst worshipp'd in my place.

—"The Abdication of Fergus MacRoy," Samuel Ferguson

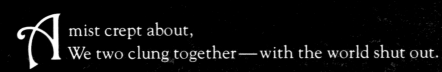

A mist crept about,
We two clung together—with the world shut out.

— "The Love-Talker," Ethna Carberry

South of Glen